# NORTH ARRAN – A Postcard Tour

## by Ken Hall

### INTRODUCTION

A great deal has been written and re-written about Arran's past. Rather than go over that familiar ground once more, this book is intended to provide a visual account of life on the island during the first half of this century. Modes of dress, transport and agricultural methods have all changed. They have been surprisingly well chronicled by old photographs and the picture postcards bought and sent by the thousands of visitors to the island since Edwardian times.

Arran, situated in the mouth of the Firth of Clyde, is about 20 miles long and 11 miles wide. To journey round the island by road is about 56 miles. The north is mountainous with many glens and streams and is sparsely populated; the south has a considerable amount of arable ground and is more akin to Ayrshire. Farming, forestry and tourism are the main sources of income. Fishing and craft industries and many other activities also make Arran a thriving and busy community.

There is also much to study on Arran. The island's archaeology, geology, botany, wildlife and history are all fascinating. But for many visitors, the outstanding beauty and tranquility alone are enough to bring them back each year.

Brodick Pier circa 1904.

Brodick Pier, the first to be built on the island, was opened in June 1872. The original wrought iron structure, shown on the front cover, was replaced by this larger and stronger wooden one in the early 1900s. Reconstruction work took place in 1946 and further strengthening was required for the island's first car ferry service which started running in June 1957. Today's roll-on roll-off facility became operational in May 1976 when the vehicle causeway was completed. Brodick is now the only ferry terminal on the east of the island. In this 1911 picture the 'Duchess of Argyll' lies alongside the pier. The warships anchored in the bay were probably on exercise in the Firth.

Brodick Port,                                          Isle of Arran.

On the north side of the pierhead, the natural harbour and old jetty lies at the mouth of the Strathwillan Burn. Behind the bridge stands the Douglas Hotel. This photograph, probably circa 1903, shows two smacks typical of the craft which were used to transport cargo across the Firth at the time. Imports would have included coal and building stone; potatoes and livestock would have been among the exports.

BRODICK HARBOUR AND BAY, ISLE OF ARRAN.    B. 2921.

This 1950 postcard, showing one of the last puffers to trade on the Clyde unloading coal, sold in large numbers to the visitors. It seems to sum up a whole era in one photograph.

In the background, below the familiar outline of Goatfell, are the grounds of Brodick Castle. Barely visible, down on the shore, is the original stone jetty, all that remains of the old village ('moved' to the other side of the bay by the 11th Duke of Hamilton).

4

Brodick Fair,
Arran.

2793. 21.

The annual fair was held at the pierhead on the first Tuesday after 20th June. The Fair Day was a general holiday and attracted special sailings from the mainland. Although its origins were as a horse and cattle fair, it also provided an opportunity for the feeing of farm workers, general trading, stalls and amusements. At the time of writing, the fate of the old ticket office and waiting-room (top centre) hangs in the balance. Although scheduled for demolition moves are afoot to save it.

INVERCLOY HOTEL, BRODICK, ISLE OF ARRAN.                    A.2646.

This inter-war Art Deco building is typical of the hotel or boarding house accommodation which was available to the many holidaymakers who came down the Clyde from Glasgow every year. At this time, in Brodick alone, there were 20 hotels, 22 guest houses and 70 furnished houses (some "without attendance")! Many farmhouses were also let out. The family would move out to a "summer house", probably at the back of the steading, or sometimes even the barn.

6

Auchrannie House, Brodick.

Auchrannie House, situated beyond the golf clubhouse at the entrance to Glen Cloy, is now surrounded by mature trees and part of the Auchrannie Hotel and Leisure complex. In the 1930s there were 15 bedrooms with H&C, terms from 35/- to 40/- per day.

Brodick Post Office, 1936. Postmaster Kasper Ribbeck (on the far right) and his staff proudly pose with four newly delivered Morris vans. The Post Office had occupied these premises from 1913 and when they moved to their present site, Pellegraini's Cafe, famous for its ice-cream, took over the building.

*The Beach and Invercloy. Regatta Day, Brodick.*

On the back of this postcard is the typical message:

23rd Aug.
1916

Alma House
Brodick,
Arran

"This is a view of the beach. You would enjoy the bathing here & boating. Margaret and Willie go home this week. Love from all. Auntie Helen."

AN ARRAN FARM, BRODICK.

This farm, on the Corrie road leading out of Brodick, is now part of the Arran Heritage Museum. There is a complex of five buildings set around a yard. Here can be found the old Rosaburn Smiddy, working once more, as well as the reconstructed old dairy and stables. There are agricultural implements from a bygone era and old farm cottage kitchen and bedroom displays. Other buildings house impressive collections of geology, archaeology and old photographs of the island.

Isle of Arran

Highland Farm, Glen Rosa

The Wrench Series No. 8082

The old township of Glenrosa, which comprised of 14 houses, was on the site of the present house and steading. In the late 18th century a variety of farming activities supported this community. Sheep and dairy cattle grazed the hillsides; oats, hay and lint were grown and some of the ground was planted with trees. However, in 1815, Robert Davidson, a progressive farmer, became sole tenant of Glen Rosa and it is still farmed by his descendants today.

Harvesters, Corriegills, Arran. The oat crop is being cut by a two-horse reaper and the bunches are being tied into sheaves with bands made from corn stalks. The lady on the reaper has the reins while the man on her left operates the tilting board with his foot and uses the rake to gather and push off the bunches. The sheaves were then stooked in groups of six or eight, left to dry in the field for two or three weeks and finally carted into a stackyard and built into corn stacks. This method was superseded in the 1930s by the binder. This implement mechanically cut and then tied the sheaves, which were later stooked by hand. In the 1950s further mechanisation resulted in the combine harvester, which cut and threshed the grain in one operation. The grain could then be carted off directly from the field, leaving the straw for the baling machine.

The Arran Estate Bothy, Brodick, Isle of Arran.

Besides farming, another important use of land on Arran was for forestry. Timber from the estate was used for fencing and building, with the surplus going for sale. A large estate such as this required a huge workforce with a wide range of talents. Joinery, horticultural and forestry skills were of particular importance.

Brodick Castle lies in the shadow of Goatfell and is surrounded by magnificent gardens and woodland. Parts of the castle date from the 14th and 16th century. Now in the care of the National Trust for Scotland, the castle was once the property of the Hamiltons. As well as the castle, its contents and gardens, the Trust also administers 7,000 acres of mountainous country which includes Goatfell and Glen Rosa.

The Summit of Goatfell, Brodick

210850 J.V.

At 2,866 ft., the mountain is not high enough (3,000 ft.) to be classed as a 'Munro'. The indicator was gifted by the Glasgow Daily Record and the base was erected by voluntary workers. According to the chart it is possible, when conditions are right, to see 122 peaks. The furthest, 105 miles away, is Skiddaw in the Lake District. Of course there are times when the weather is so bad that one cannot see anything at all! Sadly, the indicator has since been badly vandalised.

15

VIEW FROM THE SUMMIT OF
GOATFELL, ARRAN. (2866 FT.)

Some scenes have not changed over the years. Looking north-west over the Saddle, Glen Sannox is to the right with Glen Rosa to the left. The peak on the left is Cir Mor and on the skyline are the Castles and the Witches Step. This rugged and spectacular terrain is more akin to the north west of Scotland and routes range from easy hill walks to much more difficult rock climbs. There are also many pleasant walks on the lower slopes, following burns and visiting lochans, which provide excellent opportunities to observe the abundant wildlife.

IN GLEN SANNOX, ARRAN.

B7523. J.V.

This 1922 view looks up the Glen to the peak of Cir Mor on the left. In the foreground are the workings of the barytes mine. Barytes is heavy, soft and white and when milled was used as a substitute for white lead in the manufacture of paint. The mine first opened in 1839 and worked until 1862, when annual output was nearly 5,000 tons. It reopened in 1918. A new shaft was sunk and a light railway, running down to a specially constructed pier in Sannox Bay, was built. Water power from the Sannox burn was employed for the milling and screening operations. By 1934 output had risen to 9,000 tons, but the vein petered out in 1938.

Corrie from Jetty. 266/8

The road from Brodick, being almost flat, is popular with cyclists. Seals and heron can be seen on the rocks below and in the summer the roadside verges are resplendent with wild flowers, including many orchids. The village of Corrie lies approximately 6 miles north of Brodick on the shore road. The houses lie close to the shore, nestling under the "raised beaches" which rise 100 feet behind them. The quay was built for the shipment of red and white sandstone which was quarried here (there are many outcrops of red sandstone on the shore). Limestone quarries also provided employment in the area.

18

Steamers leaving Corrie

This picturesque village had no steamer pier and passengers had to be ferried ashore. Travellers with bicycles or other large pieces of baggage had to disembark at Brodick and arrange transport back to Corrie by waggonette.

Corrie, Isle of Arran.

A well-laden ferry making its way out to the steamer, with Ferry Rock in the background.

EMBARKING AT CORRIE.

BB408.J.Y.

This 1923 photograph shows the 'Duchess of Argyll' with ferryboat alongside. Steamer arrivals and departures generated a lot of local interest and many people would gather at Ferry Rock to watch the activity.

The approach to High Corrie is up a steep track. The cottages are huddled together on a plateau above the "raised beach" and form a typical "clachan" (a small village or hamlet).

Thatched Cottage, Sannox, Corrie, Isle of Arran.

Sannox village lies further along the shore to the north and has the same steep backdrop as Corrie. In Glen Sannox are very distinctive white masts which mark the measured mile used by ships on speed trials to check their performance. Many Clyde-built ships have been tested off the coast here, including the Atlantic 'Queens'. Also in the glen is an attractive 9-hole golf course. The cottage in the picture is not typical of the style of other thatched cottages on Arran, most of which were single storied.

The S. S. "Kintyre" at Loch Ranza, Isle of Arran.

E 16647

PASSENGERS
2ᴰ Each

Lochranza lies on the north west tip of Arran and is reached by road from Sannox via North Sannox and the Bou-guille Road, which rises to 650ft. The road then descends through Glen Chalmadale to the sea at Loch Ranza. The pier was opened in 1888 and all Campbeltown steamers called there on outward and return sailings from Gourock and Glasgow. After 1946 the only passenger calls were from the Gourock 'Duchesses' en route down the Kilbrannan Sound. The pier ceased to function for steamers in 1970.

At the pierhead. On disembarking, passengers gave up their tickets at the steamer gangway but, when leaving the pier itself, pier dues also had to be paid! Tuppence, as shown on the pier entrance gate, was the rate for many years. At some piers turnstiles had to be negotiated, proving most awkward if one was carrying bags and baggage!

T. S. "King Edward" at Lochranza

The 1920s saw the change from horse-drawn to motorised transport. The steamers also increased in size and power. The turbine steamer, the 'King Edward', was built in 1905. In 1972 a slipway was built, beside the old pier, to allow a car ferry service between Lochranza and Clonaig in Kintyre. The 30 minute crossing provides a useful connection for travellers to the north west coast of Scotland and the Kintyre peninsula.

Discharging Coal at Lochranza.

Lochranza Castle is mentioned in 1380, when it was regarded as one of the Royal Castles. The earliest part of the present structure dates from the latter half of the 16th century, at which time it was the stronghold of the Montgomeries. The castle stands on a green peninsula that stretches halfway across the loch, forming an inner anchorage where smacks were often beached at low tide. Goods could be unloaded straight into carts as long as the going was firm enough for the horse and its load.

Lochranza Castle, Arran

Herring fishing used to be an important island industry. In 1847 there were nearly 100 wherries (small light boats) at the herring fishing, of which 12 were from Lochranza itself. However, by 1914 there was only herring fishing from Lochranza and Pirnmill and by 1928, due to the increasing costs of bigger boats and the centralization of markets, the industry was almost extinct.

The Village, Lochranza

The decline of the fishing industry coincided with the upsurge of summer visitors and summer letting. This new source of income brought some prosperity back to the village. A golf course, a new village hall and tennis courts were added to the attractions on offer. Today Lochranza is a much more peaceful place when the summer visitors have left and the Clonaig ferry ceases to operate for the winter. This 1910 view is easily recognisable today. A few years ago the church was converted into a house and restaurant.

The Cock of Arran, the northernmost point of the island, is a large isolated mass of sandstone which rests on the beach and is a noted landmark among sailors. At one time it resembled a cock, with wings extended in the act of crowing, but the piece which represented the head has since broken off.

This road leads up through Glen Chalmadale, deteriorates into a track, rises 800 ft. and then descends to reach the ruins of The Cock Farm, which clings to the slope 300 feet above the shore. Here ex-prime minister Rt. Hon. Harold MacMillan's forebears farmed.

"Craw" Farm, Loch Ranza, Arran.

The road from Lochranza clings near to the shore as the ground rises steeply into the hills. Apart from some flat arable land at the head of Glen Catacol, there is little cultivated land until Pirnmill. The farms were basically sheep farms with a few cattle where ground enabled winter keep to be grown. The Craw Farm, perched 350 feet above the sea, looks north over Catacol Bay.

THE ROW, CATACOL, ARRAN.

Catacol, situated at the head of Catacol Glen, comprises of a row of houses, an hotel and a large sheep farm. The row of houses, built in the 1860s, were known as the "Twelve Apostles". Each has a different design of top window. They were originally intended for those people displaced by the clearances (to make way for deer not sheep). These people, however, preferred to live in other parts of the island and the houses lay empty for two years until new tenants could be found for them.

Thundergay, near Pirnmill, Isle of Arran.

E 31937

Progressing south from Catacol, Thundergay Farm and steading cling to the steep hillside above the shore road. A sign at the road end points to Coire Lochan and marks the start of a magnificent walk up into the hills. After climbing steeply behind the steading, the path follows a gushing burn to the lochan tucked away in the hills below Ben Bharrain. From the tops there are spectacular views; to the west the Mull of Kintyre, Islay, Jura and Ireland and eastwards over Loch Tanna to Goatfell, Ben Nuis and beyond.

THE OLD BOBBIN MILL, PIRNMILL, ISLE OF ARRAN   B 3003

After Thundergay the shore widens markedly and the small village of Pirnmill comes into view. The mill manufactured bobbins (or pirns) from locally grown wood. It was powered by an overshot water wheel and ran from about 1780 to 1840. The bobbins were used in the textile factories in Paisley and the mill, which supplied Clark's of Paisley, was sometimes knows as Clark's Mill.

The shoreline to the north of the village has some interesting and colourful rock structures. They are coarse, gritty, greenish-grey schists, quite a contrast to the brick red sandstone between Corrie and Brodick.

34

The Campbeltown-Greenock steamers were the most important connection with the mainland. The steamers hove-to off Machrie and Pirnmill as well as calling at Lochranza pier. This 1910 photograph shows the T.S. 'Queen Alexandra' calling at Pirnmill.

Ferry Boat, Pirnmill.

737/13

The arrival of the steamer was the highlight of the day bringing mail, bread and passengers with luggage, direct from Greenock or Glasgow. The rather primitive landing stage, long planks mounted on two large iron wheels, was kept at the water's edge.

The Ferry, Pirnmill

This large rowing boat was manned by two, or sometimes three, oarsmen and could take up to 20 passengers. From steamer to shore, depending on the wind, could take about half an hour. The ferry service from Pirnmill was operated by the Cook family, who were also involved with herring fishing and owned skiffs (small rowing boats) for drift netting.

Post Office, waiting the letters, Pirnmill, Arran.

In June 1872 a sub post office was established at Pirnmill under Greenock. At first mail was hand-stamped at both Pirnmill and Greenock; in later years the two names were found on the same circular canceller. The sub postmaster would board the steamer daily to exchange incoming for outgoing mail. Visitors were often eager for mail and would wait outside the Post Office door until it had been sorted. The girl to the left of the picture was a holidaymaker called Betty Barton. She later took up physiotherapy as a profession and married to become Mrs. Reid.

The hub of activity was around the smiddy and shop. The business, which included the smiddy, horse drawn conveyances for hire, a shop and later on a garage and a tearoom, was run by the Anderson family. Robert Anderson was a blacksmith. It was his son John who branched into the motor trade and was the first person to bring a car (a model T Ford) to the island. John was also a keen photographer and many of his photographs were made into postcards. The cards have the imprint "Andersons Series" on the back. Many of his photographic plates are on loan to the Heritage Museum. The picture on the left was taken about 1908; the lower picture dates from the 1960s.

Dwelling Houses on Golf Course, Penrioch, Pirnmill.

The original village of Penrioch was built on the hill above Pirnmill. There are now only one or two inhabited houses on this site where once was a thriving clachan. The present village of Pirnmill was mainly built in the early 1900s.

On the Golf Links, Pirnmill, Arran.

The start of this 9 hole golf course was on the shore road where the first hole was played over the football pitch. At the start of the Second World War the ground was ploughed up for agricultural use and the course was never re-opened.

Mrs. Flora Drummond, a co-founder of the suffragette movement, was born in Manchester and spent her school daysat Pirnmill. Her mother, Mrs Gibson, was a member of the Cook family, who ran the ferry there. Flora studied at the Civil Service College in Glasgow, but worked in the Telegraph Office at Pirnmill during the summer. After passing the exams to become a Post Mistress a new regulation was introduced. It required a minimum height of 5'2". Flora was 5'1". It is held that this grievance was behind her motivation to become involved with the suffragettes. She married twice. Her son by her first husband, Joseph Drummond, was named Keir Hardie after the famous Socialist leader who was vocal in support of the suffragette cause.

MRS. DRUMMOND. "VOTES FOR WOMEN."
NATIONAL WOMEN'S SOCIAL AND POLITICAL UNION,
4, CLEMENTS INN, W.C.

This campaigning scene at Pirnmill shows ferryman Mr Charlie Robertson handing over a scroll, which probably contains a large number of signatures in support of votes for women. In the driving seat is blacksmith Mr. Robert Anderson, with Mrs Flora Drummond and Mrs. Pankhurst beside him. Flora was one of the most extreme activists in the suffragette movement and was known as "The General". She even wore a badge with "General" inscribed on it!

WESTFIELD BOARDING HOUSE, PIRNMILL, ARRAN

201 144 VV

In this scene, harvesting of the softwood pine forest on the hill has just begun. The area has since been replanted.
Softwoods have also been planted along the shore to the south of Pirnmill.

44

Whitefarland Village, near Pirnmill, Isle of Arran.

Æ 31939

90 years on, the palms at Whitefarland are thriving. Palm trees grow successfully at many other places around the island, particularly Lagg and Lamlash.

ON THE ROAD BETWEEN WHITEFARLAND, AND IMACHER, PIRNMILL.    200683 J.V.

There are many more trees on this road today. To the left is the Kintyre peninsula and the stretch of water is the Kilbrannan Sound. The sheep are of the Blackface breed, which are most suited to the hill terrain and heather. There are many fine flocks of well-bred Blackface sheep on the island.

Travelling south, on the road past Whitefarland, the road gradually rises to a farm and boarding house at Imacher and then drops steeply down again to shore level. As there is another "raised beach" here, the fields along the shore have a steep backdrop. The road then reaches a fairly substantial burn called the Iorsa. Situated back from the shore, beside the river, is Dougarie Lodge. It was built in the mid 19th century, by the Duke of Hamilton, to serve as a shooting lodge. The antlers, stuck to the outside walls, have since been removed because of the water penetration they were causing.

The young Clydesdale horse is being broken in on the shore at Machrie Bay. The cart has a heavy load of gravel. The extra reins are needed to control the horse's natural tendency to run away until it has got used to the feel and the sound of the cart behind it.

Emergency on the Machrie Road! It's the early 1930s. Donald McKelvie and Mrs Shaw try to douse the flames with mud and earth while Mr Shaw takes the picture. Possibly the cause was a fractured fuel pipe.

Auchincarr Village, Machrie, Isle of Arran

This farm is frequented by many visitors as there is a byre showroom selling woollen and sheepskin products. This complements the main farm business which is producing beef cattle and sheep. Farm steadings such as this used to support numerous families and employ many workers. Today, sadly, only one family lives and works on such a location. Another attraction here is the teeming bird life. Birds of prey soar above the neighbouring crags and sandmartins are frequent summer visitors too.

Druid Stone, Machrie, Isle of Arran.

This stone can be clearly seen from the approach road to Auchincar (seen on the right of the picture). The road passes a smaller holding, with the name of Druid, which was farmed by the late "Baldy" Craig (who is shown on page 48 breaking in the young Clydesdale horse). This monolith is one of the most impressive on Arran and rises to a height of 15 feet 7 inches. The stones probably mark the positions of burial sites.

MACHRIE BAY, MACHRIE, ISLE OF ARRAN

The 9 hole golf course (on both sides of the road) was opened in 1900. This photograph was taken before the village hall and clubhouse (opened in 1934) were built. One Saturday in July is given over to the Machrie Sheep Dog Trials when the course is used for this event. Sheep dogs from the mainland and all over the island compete in this major trial which is a great attraction for visitors.

This 1913 view shows passengers boarding the ferry at Machrie. The first steamer to call here, from 1885 until 1900, was the 'Argyll'. The service restarted in 1909 and continued until 1920. Blackwaterfoot and Pirnmill were other stopping points on this route.

POST OFFICE, MACHRIE, ARRAN

Machrie is not really a village but is more an area of scattered farms and houses. The sub post office was established in 1901 after a revision of the network of services in the district. The road round the island diverges here; one road heads south to Blackwaterfoot, the other goes through the Machrie Moor, joins with the String Road and crosses the centre of the island back to Brodick.

Laggmore Boarding House, Machrie Bay.

Looking north over the bay, this boarding house stands beside one of the tracks which leads to the King's Caves, which are between Machrie and Blackwaterfoot. Machrie Bay is a wonderful place to observe sea birds such as eider ducks, teal, golden-eye, mergansers, divers, shags, cormorants and gannets. The shore itself is prolific in wild flowers including dog rose, primrose and wild violets.

*Druidical Stones, Machrie Moor*

This is an important archaeological site; at least six stone circles have been identified near the Moss Farm on the Machrie Moor. The area was probably used between 3,200 and 1,600 B.C. for worship and burial. The site is easily accessed from the road by a farm track.